Bl
THURSDAY

David Devereaux

Copyright © 2013 David Devereaux

ISBN-13: 978-1484800188
ISBN-10: 1484800184

DEDICATION

This book is dedicated to my father because he is the primary motivation behind my involvement with the motorcycle world, to my family for always supporting me no matter what I'm doing, and to my club brothers for their loyalty, honor and respect.

PHOTOS

All photos provided by Irish, my brother Twitch, and friends in the community. Thank you all.

CONTENTS

Introduction   i

PART ONE

THE MOTORCYCLE RIGHTS MOVEMENT IN
WASHINGTON STATE AND THE FIGHT
AGAINST DISCRIMINATION AND PROFILING

Chapter One   1
The Confederation of Clubs Comes To Washington
State

Chapter Two   8
2009 A Year Of Change

Chapter Three   20
2010 Bikers Gain Traction At The Capitol.

Chapter Four   32
2011 Success And Legislative Relief

Chapter Five   46
The Aftermath And The Media

Chapter Six   51
So Does The Law Work And Where Do We Go
From Here?

PART TWO

ESSAYS ADDRESSING ISSUES IMPORTANT
TO THE SURVIVAL OF MOTORCYCLE CLUB
CULTURE IN AMERICA

Essay One   57
The Elephant In The Living Room

Essay Two   59
The Day My Dad Shot Himself In The Head

Essay Three   63
The Day My Father Was Buried

Essay Four   65
The Day I Learned My Role: Speaking To The
Legislature

Essay Five   69
The NCOM Convention In Nashville: An
Influential Memory As A Prospective Patch Holder

Essay Six   74
Unification As A Path to Survival: Thoughts Of A
Second-Generation Patch Holder

Essay Seven   79
The Internet And The Future Of Motorcycle Clubs:
An Alternative To The Mainstream Media

Essay Eight   87
Is the Confederation Of Clubs And The Motorcycle
Rights Movement Worth the Effort? Survival Says
Yes.

Essay Nine   90
Why Do We Need A U.S. Defender Program When
We Already Have A Confederation Of Clubs?

Essay Ten   94
September 12, 2009: The Day A Pack Of
Motorcycles Captured Some Of Their Rights

Essay Eleven   98
December 12, 1979: A Story Of Police Corruption,
Imaginary Snitches, Planted Narcotics And Things
You Think Only Happen On Television

Essay Twelve   101
A Policy Paper Addressing The Issue Of
Motorcycle Profiling.

INTRODUCTION

Motorcycle Profiling has been occuring for a long time. The pack being harrassed in the late 1960's.

This is a story about the transformation of the motorcycle club community in Washington State and the power of motorcyclists as a grassroots political movement. This story, told through the eyes of a second-generation motorcycle club member, is about the true path to defend and help insure the survival of the community and way of life.

I named the book *Black Thursday* after the annual legislative day that takes place at the State Capitol in Olympia every January. Black Thursday coincides with the beginning of Washington's legislative session and provides a unique opportunity for motorcyclists to meet with their legislators. Also, motorcycle profiling followed us to the steps of Capitol during Black Thursday every year, until legislators could no longer ignore the blatant discrimination displayed by law enforcement. For these reasons, the name *Black Thursday* seems fitting and appropriate.

If the reader is expecting a real life 'Sons-of-Absurdity' narrative they will be sadly disappointed. This is ultimately a story about unification of motorcycle clubs in Washington State in recognition that our mutual survival depends on standing together in order to capture our rights base. So it only makes sense that I am writing for members and friends of the motorcycle club world who are more interested in their community's survival than entertaining people through sensationalized stories reinforcing stereotypes that have outlived their usefulness.

Part one tells the story of how the motorcycle rights movement in Washington State unified and mobilized into a successful constituency capable of social change and political success. Specifically, I explore the movement's efforts to obtain legislative relief in the form of legislation condemning and preventing motorcycle profiling.

Part two focuses on the broader issues facing the motorcycle club community through a series of essays examining how motorcycle clubs can survive another half-century. What traditions need to be preserved and what elements of our community threaten our survival from the inside? It is my hope that there is a little bit for everyone somewhere in the pages of this book whether your interests are political or social.

I also hope that my stories and reflections add to the momentum building in our community, to secure our rights base and adapt to new realities, so we can continue to build brotherhoods centered on freely riding motorcycles. I am always thinking about the history of motorcycle clubs and how we have gotten from there to here. Again, what are the traditions we need to preserve and what do we need to let go of in order to survive?

Clubs represent the ultimate example of the Constitutional freedoms enjoyed by Americans to express themselves and freely associate with others. Will motorcycle clubs unite based on common ground before our lifestyle becomes extinct?

This book is an attempt to answer these questions, and in some cases solutions are offered. That is why my words are directed to patch holders and the motorcycle club community.

However, if others are reading my words I hope my writing helps them understand we are simply Americans that want our basic civil liberties. I want the motorcycle club that my father helped establish to continue to flourish and excel for another half century. I share my thoughts and perspectives with this goal in mind. I hope you enjoy them.

PART ONE

THE MOTORCYCLE RIGHTS MOVEMENT IN WASHINGTON STATE AND THE FIGHT AGAINST DISCRIMINATION AND PROFILING

Motorcycles parked in front of the Capital in Olympia during Black Thursday.

Chapter One

The Confederation Of Clubs Comes To Washington State

My brother Pigpen was a major advocate of establishing a COC in Washington State.

-A Changing World-

The National Coalition of Motorcyclists, an organization born at a meeting in Las Vegas in 1986, was created in recognition of the fact that all motorcyclists are locked into a common struggle against law enforcement discrimination and profiling. Specifically, motorcycle club members were vulnerable, so NCOM organizers created the Confederation of Clubs intended to unify and mobilize the patch holder community based around common ground issues. The COC had slowly been expanding and in the mid-90's the major motorcycle clubs in Washington State decided to form a chapter. The world was changing and the COC represented recognition of this fact.

Motorcycle clubs sitting at the same table represented historical change. The COC opened lines of communication that never existed before. This represented a benefit in and of itself. Many potentially negative interactions have been adverted because the goals of a unified club community are important to leadership in almost every club in our state.

For the next 7 years the COC continued to meet and discuss ideas. Of particular concern was the clear and widespread law enforcement practice of profiling and discrimination against bikers in Washington State. However, actual and tangible gains against profiling and discrimination in both the legislature and at the grassroots level were slow to come.

Then, in 2002, an important decision in the judicial arena would serve as a primary piece of evidence that would, years later, help us in our struggle. Our COC attorney, Martin Fox, through a public disclosure request, obtained a copy of a highly inflammatory Washington State Patrol training manual entitled BASIC BIKER 101. The manual describes how to target and discriminate against motorcyclists. A Washington State Superior Court ultimately granted a permanent injunction against the use of BASIC BIKER 101 based on its unconstitutional tactics and the assertion that all bikers are dangerous. This became important because it demonstrated the paradigm and mindset of law enforcement towards bikers in Washington State.

In 2003, for the first time, the COC and ABATE gained sponsorship for a bill to address motorcycle profiling in the Washington State legislature. However, there was not a great deal of support and the motorcycle community was not mobilized. Maybe a dozen motorcycles showed up to the Capitol in 2003 and bikers were mostly uninformed about legislative issues.

In 2004, the situation remained nearly identical to the previous year. No major legislative gains were made in the arena of motorcycle rights in Washington. People weren't becoming complacent and apathetic. Just the opposite was true. The leadership in the COC knew what needed to be done. The talk and ideas needed to be followed by organized action.

-2005: I Enter the Story-

The COC and ABATE again gained sponsorship for legislation addressing motorcycle profiling in 2005. A public hearing had even been scheduled in the Senate Judiciary committee. Although there was not widespread support, at least bikers would have the opportunity to express their voice.

In January 2005, I made the decision to prospect for a motorcycle club. I'm second generation. I knew I was getting into a motorcycle club based around loyalty, honor, respect and brotherhood. What I didn't know was that within two weeks I would be testifying in front of the Washington State legislature in favor of 'A Bill to Address the Issue of Motorcycle Profiling'. Definitely not the A&E Gangland experience the general public is becoming conditioned to.

I apparently have a natural aptitude for public speaking. Pigpen, my president at the time and chair of the Confederation of Clubs, saw a role for me. I was asked to testify at the hearing. I quickly learned as much as I could and prepared to speak. The hearing went very well. Although there was majority support the committee Chair was a former law enforcement officer and the bill was killed.

Despite this failure something was sparked. A motivation to fight discrimination and profiling against the motorcycle club community became a clear and driving goal, almost from the beginning of my involvement in a motorcycle club. To this day, I feel a personal obligation to continue this fight in order to ensure that the motorcycle club community continues to survive. We must continue to unify for the purpose of securing our rights to freedom of expression, peaceful assemble, due process, lawful search and seizure and our equal protections granted by the US Constitution.

The struggle for survival of the motorcycle club community as we know it is not a 'Look, the sky is falling!' fairy tale. Motorcycle clubs are under attack at many levels. The number of large-scale and extravagant investigations and indictments are growing. Many of these indictments end in futility, but the monetary and perceptual damage is many times irreversible. The strategies being employed to target motorcycle clubs are innovative and widespread. The only relevant question is what motorcycle clubs are going to do about it? Will we continue to be the victims of discrimination and profiling *or* will we unify around our mutual political goals? Will we fight back in order to demand and secure our rights base?

That day back in the winter of 2005 answered these questions for me. So started a seven-year struggle to obtain legislative relief in the form of a bill addressing the issue of motorcycle profiling in Washington State. It is my hope that motorcycle clubs in other states can apply what we have learned in their own states. I ultimately envision a mobilized and powerful motorcycle rights movement that spans the entire United States.

In 2005, the motorcycle rights movement in Washington State consisted of separate entities only

Speaking at the May Motorcycle Awareness Rally on the steps of the Oregon Capitol.

partially communicating or working together. On one side was the COC (consisting of motorcycle clubs) and on the other side was ABATE (mainly independents). There was definitely a huge divide between these two communities, despite the fact that there was an ABATE liaison to the COC, and club members had originally started ABATE in Washington. There were many reasons for this divide, but most of them came down to ABATE leadership's inability to relate to the clubs.

In 2006 and 2007 the story was much the same, except that the bill didn't even receive a hearing. The rift between the COC and ABATE continued to deteriorate, and the organizations were nowhere close to being on the same page. ABATE was concerned with left-hand turn legislation while the COC remained steadfast in its pursuit of a bill to address motorcycle profiling.

The next year I learned that the old cliché is true. If you want it done right (or done at all!) most of the time you have to do it yourself. No one had done anything to obtain sponsorship for the profiling bill and it was very late in a short session before we found this out. I had learned enough to attempt to find a sponsor and start the process, but ultimately time was the enemy.

However, I understood how the system worked and the clubs in the COC were not losing enthusiasm. For so long there was only talk and now members of the COC, with real capabilities, were doing something themselves. The effect was contagious and things were about to change in Washington State .

Chapter Two

2009 A Year Of Change

Gathering before the Washington COC protest run 2009. A day that helped ignite the movement to end profiling in Washington.

-January-

The motorcycle rights movement began to change in 2009. Suddenly I felt a huge amount of support and enthusiasm that I hadn't felt before. Also, a few of my brothers began to get very involved in the COC, and things were starting to become a little more organized. Clear indications of change came early in the year.

Black Thursday, the annual legislative day for bikers at the Capitol, takes place in January. There seemed to be more interest this year so we planned on meeting and riding into the Capitol as a Confederation. I had been attending Black Thursday since 2005 and never seen more than 25 bikes attend. This year would be very different.

For the first time in years more than a hundred bikes showed up to ride into the Capitol together. I felt incredibly proud leading that pack and will always remember my brother Pigpen waiting and cheering for the pack as it rolled through the campus.

We pulled into the parking lot and were directed to a side lot next to a huge hedge of bushes. Little did we know that the most important catalyst for widespread support for a profiling bill in the legislature was about to occur. As we parked and made our way to the Capitol building, in pursuit of a sponsor for a bill to address motorcycle discrimination, the Washington State Patrol was about to demonstrate why motorcyclists required legislative relief.

A Washington State trooper caught in the bushes profiling every motorcyclist at the Capital during Black Thursday 2009.

Indeed, motorcycle profiling by Washington State law enforcement had followed us to the steps of the Capitol. While motorcyclists were seeking relief against profiling inside, the Washington State Patrol was in the parking lot, being captured on videotape crawling through the bushes, recording the license plate numbers and identifying information of every motorcycle in the parking lot. Word quickly spread and I immediately knew this incident could become critical to our movement.

I made arrangements to get a copy of the video hoping it was preserved. I also hoped that it looked as egregious as it sounded. I couldn't imagine legislators tolerating this kind of blatant discrimination on the grounds of the Capitol once they could watch it happen with their own eyes. It turned out to be an incredible visual demonstration of discrimination and profiling against motorcyclists in Washington State.

Our COC attorney wrote a letter to the Governor and copied the Chief of the Washington State Patrol complaining of this obviously outrageous behavior. The Chief Batiste responded that the trooper was gathering information on motorcycles based on the belief that there is a high propensity for violence when motorcycle clubs gather. The preemptive information gathering would therefore give the State Patrol a complete list of potential witnesses in case of violence. Incredible. The Chief of the State Patrol was, in writing, articulating and justifying law enforcement's paradigm of discrimination and profiling.

Moreover, this incident solidified the importance of visual documentation in the form of pictures and video. From this point forward, there has been video and photographic documentation of every important COC event in Washington State. This incident also highlighted the critical importance of documented and official correspondence. A mistake made in writing cannot be denied or refuted and serves as excellent evidence in both the judicial and legislative arenas.

Momentum was gaining. Enthusiasm and support were continuing to grow. There were now members of the COC that possessed the necessary skills to document the evidence and present a coherent story to legislators. The final piece of the puzzle was about to be revealed.

-February-

In February, the US Defender program was introduced to the Northwest. The program's creator, Gimmie Jimmie, flew out from Texas to talk to the Washington State COC about the possibility of starting the program in our state. This program turned out to be the piece we needed to complete an efficient and functioning motorcycle rights movement in Washington State.

The COC US Defenders program is an ingenious but simple concept. The US Defenders is essentially a networking of clubs and organizations allowing near instantaneous communication and requests for action.

Each participating state chooses a Commander and Lt. Commander to organize, run, and publicly represent the organization in their state. Each participating organization offers a Defender and an alternate. Defenders are responsible for monitoring their Emails on a daily basis and communicating any calls to action back to their organizations.

Initially, there were objections to the program. Some clubs were concerned that the US Defenders was just a way for clubs to control and influence other clubs. It was clear that there was interest. But it was also clear that everyone had to talk it out before the program would work. I was convinced that these objections could be answered.

-March-

The first COC meeting after our introduction to the US Defenders program made it clear that any concerns could easily be overcome. Washington was already motivated and the US Defenders seemed like the tool we needed to fully mobilize. The COC representatives that had gotten all the clubs to sit at the same table were now going to stand side-by-side *and* get something done.

Washington State decided to participate in the US Defenders program and it has turned out to be the glue that binds all of the different elements of our previously fractured motorcycle rights movement together. I was elected Commander of the program because of my public speaking and argumentation skills. Our Lt. Commander, Lucky Les, is an expert at organization and networking, and had an implementation plan prepared and ready to execute. Every organization offered a Defender and an alternate . Our program was complete.

The US Defenders provided a structure that was highly organized, being represented by the best public speaker in our community, with instantaneous communication and support from every participating motorcycle club in Washington State.

-April-

With all this momentum and excitement it was time to see if the US Defenders program would help the COC in Washington State. I prepared a pre-formatted and pre-addressed letter to our US Senators voicing our objections to an overly broad anti-gang bill that was being proposed in 2009. A letter writing campaign seemed to be a simple test to determine if a Call To Action (CTA) from the US Defenders in Washington would work, in terms of instantaneous communication and a rapid response.

The Washington COC was able to amass approximately 1,200 letters within one week. Every participating organization responded. The few kinks in the process were being worked out and it was obvious the US Defenders program would be a powerful asset to the COC.

The COC made the decision to open membership in the US Defenders program to any non-law enforcement motorcycle organization that was interested in participating in a rights-based movement. The decision to open membership to non-COC clubs and organizations would help bridge the gap between independent bikers and club members in Washington State. For example, ABATE and numerous motorcycle rights organizations are involved in the US Defenders and this has helped a previously fractured movement to be more cohesive.

-May through August-

Washington continued to expand membership and understanding of the US Defenders. I spoke with several organizations and clubs explaining the structure and how everything worked. I spoke with ABATE's Board of Directors to ensure that the leadership understood that the US Defenders was not a plan by club members to take over or influence their organization.

Lessons learned from the first CTA were applied and our handle on the program came fairly quick. As the summer came to a close it was time to use the US Defenders as a tool to obtain a small piece of our rights base through immediate grassroots action.

-September-

Numerous establishments in the Northwest had recently adopted 'no motorcycle club colors' policies and members of the COC were being denied access. I came up with the idea of having a protest run to a couple of these establishments as a way to demonstrate that the US Defenders program could make a difference.

The idea was straightforward and direct. Send out a CTA requesting that all available motorcyclists and motorcycle club members meet at the Lighthouse Tavern in Everett. The Lighthouse is biker-friendly and provided a good staging area and starting point. The establishments to be protested were not announced until we were ready to leave the Lighthouse in order to maintain the element of surprise. This ended up working well because we were able to peacefully overwhelm each establishment without being stopped at the door by the owner or being stopped in the parking lot by law enforcement.

Over 200 motorcycles showed that day. It was truly amazing and inspiring to see members of almost every club in Washington State riding together with the common purpose of equality and freedom. It was equally inspiring to have a completely successful result with absolutely not a single negative incident.

With the visible support of nearly 200 bikers I presented the owners of 2 establishments with the irrefutable truth: Denying equal access to motorcyclists violates our first amendment rights to expression and our fourteenth amendment equal protections. I gave a copy of the following letter to each establishment.

September 12, 2009

Attention Management,

The Washington State Confederation of Clubs has recently been made aware that your establishment has recently practiced the policy of denying motorcycle club members entrance and/or service if they are wearing their club colors. This practice is based on discriminatory stereotyping blatantly violating the First and Fourteenth Amendments of the U.S. Constitution. Your right to 'deny service to anyone' does not include discrimination against the basic freedom of expression even if it is based on the belief that motorcycle club members wearing colors may result in unrest. Absent tangible, specific and empirical examples there is no basis for denying access to an entire class of American and Washington State citizens.

The Washington State Confederation of Clubs respectfully requests that your establishment permanently discontinue the practice of denying motorcycle club members access or service. The Confederation represents a massive constituency and we are determined to gain access to our rights base at every level through legitimate protest and political activism.

Any questions or inquiries may be directed to Martin Fox, attorney for the Washington State Confederation of Clubs.

Faced with this irrefutable truth, both establishments agreed to serve bikers that day and changed their policies. These establishments are still regularly monitored by the COC ensuring that these changes remain permanent.

This protest run has been critical for two reasons. First, the protest proved to everyone that the US Defender program worked. Over 200 bikers were mobilized, organized and achieved success. This has generated a more serious and long lasting commitment from everyone involved. Second, this protest proved that we could achieve our goals through unity and destroy the myth that motorcycle clubs are violent when they gather. Tangible change was achieved through peaceful grassroots political activism and everyone present was directly involved in the process and ultimate success.

Meeting with Representative Steve Kirby in late 2009 securing a primary sponsor for a motorcycle profiling bill. My brother Twitch (far left) and Mr. Breeze (to the right of me) are heavily involved in the motorcycle rights movement.

-October through December-

The 2010 legislative session was fast approaching and the COC was determined to have success passing a bill addressing the issue of motorcycle profiling. Also, a new legislative representative for ABATE was appointed. Refreshingly, Mr. Breeze seemed to be on the same page as the COC. Also, Irish McKinney became the new ABATE liaison to the COC and successfully bridged the gap between independents and club members. For the first time, ABATE agreed to adopt the same legislative agenda as the COC. In the past, the profiling effort was largely perceived by ABATE as a club issue. ABATE was committed.

A meeting was arranged with Representative Steve Kirby, 29th legislative district, to discuss the possibility of sponsoring legislation. The meeting went very well. A few of us were able to share our stories and experience. Representative Kirby was on-board. He made no promises of success, but he did promise to push the legislation.

Everything was in place for the new session. We had sponsorship in the House and Black Thursday was just around the corner. We were armed with evidence and focused on success at the legislature in 2010.

Chapter Three

2010 Bikers Gain Traction At The Capitol

US Defenders gathered in front of the Capital.

-Black Thursday-

In 2010, the motorcycle rights movement in Washington was reinvigorated and mobilized. On January 21, 2010 another COC pack of over 200 motorcycles arrived at the Capitol with a clear agenda and purpose. This was the largest COC pack in the history of Black Thursday, and the energy level and feeling of unity was unparalleled. When we arrived at the Capitol we had designated parking and law enforcement was waiting and showing force.

Although we didn't catch them crawling through the bushes like we did in 2009, the motorcycle rights constituency did have to endure a massive amount of law enforcement scrutiny. In fact, we had to walk through a virtual gauntlet of law enforcement personnel and vehicles, including a K9 unit, before we could reach the steps of the Capitol.

This blatant discrimination and misappropriation of public resources was truly an outrage. But again, we had learned the power of the visual so we just added the video and picture documentation to our growing war chest of evidence demonstrating a clear pattern of motorcycle profiling.

Primary sponsorship was secured in the House of Representatives so the COC and ABATE decided to focus on two goals during Black Thursday 2010. First, continue to generate support in the House of Representatives urging a public hearing. Second, try to obtain a primary sponsor for a bill in the Senate. The legislative session would only last 60 days so our work was cut out for us.

In terms of gaining more support, we had success in the House of Representatives. Indeed, nearly every Representative said they were in support of HB 2511, "A Bill Addressing The Issue of Motorcycle Profiling". It also appeared that Representative Christopher Hurst, Chairman of the Public Safety and Emergency Preparedness (PSEP) committee, was going to schedule a public hearing. It looked like the bill might have some traction. However, the Senate was a different story. Gaining sponsorship in this chamber of Congress proved to be more difficult.

A meeting had been previously arranged with a longtime Republican Senator for the express intent of obtaining sponsorship for a companion bill addressing motorcycle profiling in the Senate. However, the meeting turned out to be an ambush of sorts. That is my perception. The Senator had invited three spokesmen from three Washington law enforcement agencies. The Senator asked that all recording devices be turned off. The Senator decided that the issues related to motorcycle profiling could best be addressed through dialogue instead of legislation. Her assessment was incorrect.

I was fairly certain that no dialogue would be possible. Law enforcement is largely ignorant about motorcycle clubs yet are very committed to their outdated conceptual framework. However, I was allowed to start the dialogue and looked forward to the opportunity to dismantle the opposition's specious assumptions.

I began to articulate the evidence demonstrating a clear pattern of motorcycle profiling and the need for legislative relief. After about a minute one of the spokesman became visibly upset, came out of his chair and blurted, "Do you think we're stupid? Don't you think we know who you guys are? We know what you've been doing since the '70's!"

Obviously, these were rhetorical questions and emotional statements about a time pre-dating my own age of reason. But they clearly demonstrated our point and I seized the opportunity.

I looked at the Senator and said, "If they treat us this way in front of a Senator, how do you think they treat us when you're not around? They crawl through the bushes obtaining information and conducting investigations based on an outdated stereotype. Law enforcement doesn't even have enough respect to refrain from discrimination and profiling on the grounds of the state Capitol." The tone of the meeting was changing.

It was clear that this was a confrontational dialogue at best. I was very prepared and very convicted. I was also able to articulate myself more clearly than the under-prepared opposition. Unfortunately, I was also unsuccessful obtaining sponsorship from the Senator.

Regardless of how clear the case was for legislative relief, the Senator was not interested in sponsorship. Her attempt at arbitration had failed. Law enforcement had no credible argument. Despite all of this, the Senator told us that she didn't think that HB 2511 would go anywhere in the House. She said the bill had no support. How wrong she turned out to be.

Ironically, she ended up voting for the same bill in 2011. She has since convinced herself that she is a friend of the motorcycle constituency. As long as she continues to support our efforts in the future, I am fine with whatever version of reality the Senator chooses to embrace.

-HB 2511: A Bill to Address the Issue of Motorcycle Profiling-

A bill addressing motorcycle profiling had received sponsorship in the past. The bill had even had public hearings as far back as 2003. But a bill to address the issue of motorcycle profiling had never made it past a committee. History was about to be made.

In February, a public hearing in front of the PSEP committee was scheduled. As the spokesperson for the Confederation of Clubs and US Defenders, I was prepared to testify. Mr. Breeze was also going to testify on behalf of ABATE and independent motorcyclists in Washington State. I spoke first.

I began by defining motorcycle profiling and explaining its legal and legislative roots. I then established a clear case that the entire motorcycle community was being profiled based on documented proof that law enforcement believes motorcycle club members are more likely than others to be violent or

HB 2511 - MOTORCYCLE PROFILING 2/2/10
PUBLIC HEARING
FOR MORE INFORMATION VISIT WWW.LEG.WA.GOV
HOUSE PUBLIC SAFETY & EMERGENCY PREPAREDNESS CMTE.

Testifyting in front of the House in 2010.

commit crimes. This is true from the streets we ride on, to the steps of the Capitol, and the bushes we park our motorcycles in front of.

I then explained how law enforcement was training each other to discriminate against bikers with a concept called BASIC BIKER 101. I produced the manual and the accompanying Superior Court permanent injunction granted against BASIC BIKER 101 in 2002.

I produced testimony from a recent case where our COC attorney brilliantly cross-examined a state trooper getting him to admit that BASIC BIKER 101 tactics are how troopers are taught to deal with bikers. Importantly, the trooper also admitted to knowing nothing about the injunction that had been granted 7 years prior. The fact that the trooper's admissions had occurred only 3 months before to my testimony had an impact.

Establishing the case for legislative relief becomes easier when judicial reprimands are repeatedly ignored by law enforcement. Indeed, the possibility of civil suits on the horizon during a recession amounts to being a persuasive argument.

Finally, I directly addressed questions related to gangs and gang legislation. I explained that the 'Sons of Absurdity' stereotype has outlived its usefulness. Most club members are average Americans with jobs and families. Criminal activity in motorcycle clubs, like law enforcement, is generally isolated and represents the actions of an individual. Obviously, the actions of an individual should not define an entire class of people.

I also familiarized the committee with State v. Ladson (1999), the Washington State Supreme Court precedent defining pre-textual traffic stops as unconstitutional based on Article I, Section 7 privacy protections. I reminded the committee that Ladson involved officers on proactive gang patrol, and the suspects were suspected drug dealers. In other words, even if we were all gangs profiling is still unconstitutional. Traffic code should not be used to conduct criminal investigations when there would otherwise be insufficient evident to obtain a criminal warrant.

My testimony was very well received. In fact, the committee moved into Executive Session and reported the bill out of committee with a do-pass recommendation on the spot. We were told that this was unusual, but based on the strength of the testimony the discussion of motorcycle profiling deserved to continue.

For the first time in the history of Washington State, or any other state for that matter, a bill to address the issue of motorcycle profiling had made it past a policy committee. A week later the bill passed the House of Representatives by a vote of 96-2 and was on its way to the Senate. It was a short 60-day session but there was time if we moved quickly.

The US Defenders sent out another CTA urging members of the Senate Judiciary committee to schedule a hearing on HB 2511. A few days later the bill was added to the agenda of the final Judiciary hearing scheduled for the 2010 session. It seemed like the bill had a chance of passing into law. But this was politics and we all know that anything can happen.

Less than 24 hours before the scheduled public hearing HB 2511 was removed from the agenda and replaced with a budget bill from the Governor's office. Despite all of our hard work and momentum the bill was killed in committee.

I picked myself up, gathered my strength and planned to move ahead. We were so close. Next year I was determined to succeed. I was not going to quit and I was not going to accept anything less than a law that condemned and prevented motorcycle profiling.

-The Rest of 2010 and the Annual Protest Run-

The remainder of 2010 was spent planning strategy for 2011 and a protest run scheduled for September 11th. This would be exactly one year after the COC's first protest run that had proven so successful.

This time we were focused on an establishment in my hometown, Tacoma. The Swiss had long been a Tacoma icon and served patch holders for years. Suddenly the policy had changed and I felt it needed to be changed back.

In the early afternoon of September 11th nearly 200 club members from almost every club in Washington gathered at the 48 street Pub in Tacoma in preparation for our protest of the Swiss's 'No Cuts' policy.

The pack made the short ride to the Swiss without incident. I, along with our COC attorney Martin Fox, entered the Swiss. Immediately the owner approached and asked what we wanted. He told us there was a 'no motorcycle cuts' policy and we weren't allowed inside. I told him that that was exactly what I had come to discuss with him. He followed us outside.

Once outside he was surprised to see nearly 200 club members waiting to be served. I began by explaining that the Swiss's 'no motorcycle cuts' policy was unconstitutional and violated the First and Fourteenth Amendments of the US Constitution. I also provided him with the written statement that I had

Successfully convincing the owner of the Swiss to lift the 'no motorcycle colors' policy in 2010.

developed a year earlier that explains our position and determination to capture our rights base through all legal and political mechanisms available. I calmly and precisely answered all of his objections. I explained that his beliefs were based on outdated stereotypes. I repeatedly asked him to allow us in because it was just the right thing to do. He'd certainly make money.

Our attorney suggested he grant a one-day moratorium. This would give us a chance to prove that the myth was false. He eventually caved and allowed us in.

This was another success and the unity and momentum of the COC in Washington was at an all-time high. The change at the Swiss became permanent and motorcycle colors and cuts are allowed to this day.

The official promo poster for the documentary film,
"What It's All About"

Pigpen, Twitch, and myself in Indy. 'What Its All
About' received the Silver Spoke Media Award at
NCOM in 2012.

-2010: The Year of the Documentary-

Of significant note in 2010 was the creation of a documentary created by my brother Twitch called, "What It's All About." The documentary covers the events mobilizing the motorcycle rights movement in Washington State in 2009 and 2010. I'm extremely proud of Twitch because the final product documents a story I have been a part of and the story could not have been told any better.

This film has also serves as proof that visually documenting our struggle against profiling and discrimination can help mobilize motorcyclists everywhere. Twitch has distributed copies of the documentary all over the country, including Hawaii. This film effectively tells the story of the motorcycle rights movement in Washington State and people are interested.

My hope is that Twitch, and others, will continue to develop documentaries because I think they are an incredible tool in the fight for freedoms and a secure rights base. The media machine that makes millions off of exploiting the outlaw biker stereotype does not control independent film productions so motorcyclists can tell their stories without interference.

Chapter Four

2011 Success And Legislative Relief

The steps of the Capitol during Black Thursday 2011.

-Black Thursday-

2011 was a unique experience for the motorcycle constituency at the Washington State legislature. For the first time in years there was no visible law enforcement presence or harassment when the pack arrived for Black Thursday. We also had primary sponsorship for a bill to address motorcycle profiling. Things were changing and it seemed like the motorcycle rights movement was ahead of the curve and poised for success.

In terms of law enforcement presence, there was a noticeable difference compared to the last few years. We caught no one crawling through the bushes and there was no gauntlet to pass through before reaching the steps of the Capitol. It was just another day in Olympia.

On this day, motorcyclists were an organized and mobilized constituency, determined to protect *their* rights base, showing up on *their* annual legislative day, determined to advance and protect *their* community free from open and blatant profiling and discrimination. In fact, our goal is to experience this noticeable change in law enforcement behavior and practice outside the sanctity of the Capitol and watchful legislators.

The prospects for success on the legislative front also seemed very bright. In a long list of things that were happening for the first time, the motorcycle profiling bill had a dozen sponsors in both the House and Senate and ABATE's surveys indicated no legislative opposition.

-Public Hearings and the Legislative Session-

Very quickly we had two public hearings scheduled. The first was on February 2, for HB 1333, in front of the House committee on Public Safety and Emergency Preparedness. The very next day was a hearing in front of the Senate Judiciary committee on the Senate version of the bill SB 5242. Things seemed to be moving along much smoother than in the past.

Companion bills meant that the issue of motorcycle profiling would be on every legislator's mind. Companion bills also meant that there was double the chance of success.

The US Defenders sent out a call to action requesting that all available motorcyclists show up to hearings in order to demonstrate visible support. I was designated to testify on behalf of the COC and the US Defenders. Mr. Breeze was testifying on behalf of ABATE and independent motorcyclists in our state. We were both very prepared. The US Defenders program again showed its worth. Both hearings were packed with club members and independents and the sense of purpose and unity was unmistakable.

The first hearing in the House would be different than 2010. Last year the PSEP committee had never heard me testify and I had to lay out the entire argument with intensity and pin-point accuracy. In 2011, six members of the committee were sponsors to the bill. This included the chair of the committee, Representative Christopher Hurst. Also, the bill passed the House 96-2 in 2010, so the legislation had traction. I focused on the incidents that had occurred since the previous year, and confidently argued that passing HB 1333 into law was just the right thing to do.

Specifically, I focused on a recent $90,000 stipulated judgment against the State Patrol for discrimination and profiling a motorcycle club member. Indeed, making reference to last year's testimony, I reminded the committee that the trooper involved was the same trooper that admitted, under oath, to using BASIC BIKER 101 tactics regardless of an injunction.

This hearing turned out to be more of a formality because we had so much support. However, this hearing turned out to be important because it gave me a chance to hear the Washington Association of Sheriffs and Police Chiefs testify in opposition to the bill.

The policy director for the WASPC testified that the bill would ultimately have a 2.7 million dollar impact to local governments and agencies. The PSEP was not persuaded and HB 1333 was given a unanimous do pass recommendation. However, this opportunity to hear the opposition put me in an excellent strategic position for tomorrow's hearing in the Senate. History shows that ridiculous fiscal notes have been known to kill viable legislation, despite their absurdity. The Senate Judiciary had never heard me testify and I was determined to hit a home run. Failure was simply not an option. Too many people were counting on me.

The Senate hearing the next day turned out to be even better than I anticipated. I was given the opportunity to speak first and I had been visualizing this opportunity for months. Indeed, I was effective and compelling enough that Senator Klein, the chair of the Judiciary, forgot to turn the timer on and I was able to testify for over 12 minutes. I was able to thoroughly articulate a justification for legislative relief. More importantly, I was able to on-point answer and defeat every argument WASPC had presented the day before.

This pre-emption appeared to completely frazzle the WASPC policy director and she actually agreed with my analysis during her testimony. Senator Hargrove, the primary sponsor, informed her that every Senator present thought WASPC's fiscal analysis was "bogus". These hearings are a matter of record and are available for anyone to view.

It truly was satisfying. It was clear that I had communicated to the Judiciary and they were impressed and supportive. I was asked what law school I went to and was thanked for my preparedness. I admit this all felt very good. But most importantly, with all ego aside, we achieved our goal. SB 5242 was given yet another unanimous do-pass recommendation and for the first time a bill to address motorcycle profiling was headed to the floor of the Senate after a short stop in Rules.

On February 4th we were thrown a curveball in the House. Instead of being referred directly to Rules,

HB 1333 was sent to Appropriations instead. Because WASPC had asserted such a huge fiscal impact the PSEP committee felt Appropriations analysis was important.

Regardless of truth, even a false fiscal report can delay and kill perfectly functional and necessary legislation. Again, the US Defenders sent out a call to action requesting a public hearing in the House Appropriations committee. Again, the US Defenders were successful and a public hearing was scheduled for February.

The hearing in Appropriations was different than previous hearings in front of policy committees. Appropriations focuses on fiscal considerations and policy arguments are considered only if they relate or outweigh fiscal concerns. The assertion that this bill would cost local governments 2.7 million dollars required that we completely dismantle the claim if there was any hope of success in the middle of a recession. I researched WASPC's fiscal claims and prepared an on-point refutation of every specious claim.

Merely integrating a policy statement and training into current policies and procedures would have zero economic impact. Also, the costs of not addressing motorcycle profiling were continuing to proliferate. I felt confidant that I would be able to provide a superior and more persuasive cost benefit analysis than WASPC. WASPC had already proven that they were under-prepared and not even moderately persuasive to legislators in the face of overwhelming evidence of widespread profiling. There was no reason to assume that things would be any different this time around.

The Appropriations hearing presented an opportunity for a direct and in-depth attack on the basis of WASPC's claims. The fact that WASPC represented fiscal costs as additive was false and intentionally misleading. Integration into current policies on racial profiling would actually be cost free and have zero budgetary impact. In other words, WASPC's fiscal analysis was was nothing more than smoke and mirrors.

WASPC sent the policy director's boss to testify in her place. Obviously WASPC not been successful up to this point. As it turned out, the policy director was much better and WASPC should have probably had her testify again. The only thing that was clear was that WASPC did not support this bill. In my opinion, the opposition represented a massive waste of public resources only costing the state of Washington. Taxes pay WASPC's salary base and these people are supposed to be prepared. WASPC was not.

A few days later Appropriations gave HB 1333 a unanimous do-pass recommendation. However, there was a catch. WASPC proposed an amendment that was introduced during an Executive Session, not the public hearing. The amendment just clarified that training would be integrated into current policies and procedures. This eliminated fiscal concerns. But WASPC's amendment also changed the fundamental definition of motorcycle profiling and stripped away essential language.

WASPC's definition confined profiling to incidents that occur only when an individual is operating a motorcycle. This definition was overly restrictive and inconsistent with current legal definitions of profiling. Also, many incidents occur when we are not on our motorcycles. Profiling at the Capitol on Black Thursday demonstrates this truth. Again, the US Defenders initiated another call to action requesting a floor amendment to correct the definition.

Within 24 hours we had a representative file a floor amendment correcting the definition, once again proving that ABATE and the COC were very effective when mobilized through the US Defenders. This experience serves as a reminder that anything can happen in politics so it is very important to constantly monitor legislation even when all seems to be going well.

Everything seemed to be on track and dialed in. The initial cutoff period for bills in the house of origin was approaching and both HB 1333 and SB 5242 were in Rules waiting to be placed on their respective floor calendars. We were given assurances that both bills would be pulled from Rules and ultimately the Senate came through first.

On March 5, 2011 the Senate unanimously (48-0-0-1) voted in favor of a bill addressing the issue of motorcycle profiling. Another floor amendment was offered, but this time it was offered by Senator Hargrove, the bills primary sponsor. Hargrove's amendment was exactly what the motorcycle constituency wanted. Enjoined Senate Bill 5242 (ESB 5242) required law enforcement to adopt a policy statement condemning motorcycle profiling and integrate training into current efforts to address profiling. Importantly, Hargrove's amendment preserved the original definition of motorcycle profiling, modeled after the definition of racial profiling, which more fully addresses the broad scope of profiling incidents.

Another first. Now a bill addressing motorcycle profiling had passed both chambers of the state legislature in consecutive years. At this point the focus became the Senate's version of the bill because it had passed first. The companion bill, HB 1333, sat in rules and missed the cutoff period. Now all we had to do was pass ESB 5242 through the House of Representatives. I felt very confident that success was just around the corner.

Remember, the bill had already had two hearings in front of the PSEP committee and both were extremely favorable. Six committee members were sponsors to the companion bill and were supportive of the COC and ABATE's efforts. There was nothing left to do but wait for the PSEP committee to schedule a hearing.

So wait is what everyone involved did. I started to get nervous. ABATE's legislative representative and I drafted and sent letters to every member of the PSEP committee. It was March 10th and the final cut-off date was March 25th. By March 15th we had received no response. Apparently the US Defenders needed to be activated. The final cutoff period was fast approaching so the US Defenders sent out another call to action requesting that the PSEP committee schedule a public hearing.

Why had no hearing been scheduled? On Saturday March 19th the answer became apparent as responses to the call to action began pouring in. According to chairman Hurst, members of ABATE contacted his office after ESB 5242 passed the Senate and requested that a hearing not be scheduled because the wording of the Senate's version was not in line with the goals of ABATE. Representative Hurst confirmed that other committee members had been contacted. Unfortunately, a hearing could no longer be scheduled due to the 5-day public notice requirement. Chairman Hurst assured us that this bill would move next year and was sorry for the misunderstanding.

I was in shock! Who contacted a Representative and said we didn't support the Senate's version of the bill? I couldn't really believe that this was happening. All of the hard work and dedication was apparently being sabotaged by the misinformed voice of some unknown ABATE members. ABATE leadership was equally outraged and concerned that this could damage (and maybe even reverse) the progress made unifying the club and independent segments of the community. I was determined to not let everything unravel. There had to be a way around the 5-day notice requirement for a bill that had such overwhelming support. So I did a little research and found a way.

I began reading through the rules governing the House of Representatives. I found what I was looking for under House Rule 24. An exception to the 5-day notice requirement can be granted in cases that demand it , including issues that have previously been heard in committee. With the Speaker of the House's approval a hearing could be scheduled.

Again, in cooperation with ABATE, letters were drafted and sent to Chairman Hurst and the other PSEP committee members. The exceptions to the 5-day notice requirement were articulated. We requested that a hearing be scheduled considering the circumstances and the constitutional implications of profiling legislation.

Amazingly, Chairman Hurst responded to our requests and research and scheduled a public hearing for ESB 5242 to take place the next day, Tuesday March 22. I was determined to have success now that we were back in the game. Also, I would be testifying alone because ABATE's legislative representative was unavailable on such short notice. I was prepared to complete this journey and anxious to get it done.

The US Defenders sent out a call to action requesting presence at the hearing and there wasn't an empty chair. The hearing in front of the PSEP committee was the third I had testified in over the last 2 years. This hearing was concise and to the point. I primarily focused on the fiscal illusions advanced by WASPC in an attempt to keep the bill out of Appropriations. It really felt amazing to know I had the support of every Representative on the committee.

WASPC didn't even testify in opposition this time. A bill addressing the issue of motorcycle profiling received another unanimous do-pass recommendation and was hopefully on the way to the floor via the Rules committee.

-The Final Steps-

The sun continued to shine on us. ESB 5242 was referred to rules avoiding the Appropriations death trap. I decided that a final push from the US Defenders could help seal the deal. The Rules committee was planning on meeting Thursday March 31st and it was a good opportunity to request that ESB 5242 be pulled to the floor calendar. A call to action was issued early Thursday and by noon ESB 5242 was pulled to the floor of the House and scheduled for a Second Reading. The US Defenders issued a final call to action Friday morning urging that every representative vote in favor of ESB 5242.

I am confidant that the legislature heard the COC, ABATE and the US Defenders. On Friday afternoon, April 1, 2011, the Washington State House of Representatives unanimously passed ESB 5242. This marked the first time in history a motorcycle profiling bill has passed both chambers of any state legislature the same year and completed the journey into law. ESB 5242 unanimously passed the Senate and the House so the Governor could not have vetoed the bill even if she had wanted to.

Meeting with Rep. Steve Kirby a few minutes before the motorcycle profiling bill signing ceremony.

Indeed, on April 13th, 2011 Governor Gregoire signed ESB 5242, a bill addressing the issue of motorcycle profiling, into law. The sensationalized view of the motorcycle community propagated by the media and law enforcement is completely untrue and has outlived its usefulness. I felt proud standing in the Governor's office with Pigpen, Twitch, Lucky Les, Mr. Breeze and every biker who showed up that day, as we all watched history being made with a signature. We have all worked so hard and our efforts had finally paid off.

This bill provides the necessary training and legal protections to substantially reduce motorcycle profiling in Washington State. The law, modeled after the racial profiling legislation passed in 2002, gives motorcyclists the same type of constitutional protection against law enforcement discrimination and profiling granted other classes. This is truly an historical success for motorcyclists.

Specifically, the bill requires all law enforcement in Washington State to adopt a written policy condemning motorcycle profiling and mandates that the Criminal Justice Training Commission address the issue of motorcycle profiling in required basic law enforcement training courses.

The final section of the bill defines motorcycle profiling as "the illegal use of the fact that a person rides a motorcycle or wears motorcycle-related paraphernalia as a factor in deciding to stop and question, take enforcement action, arrest, or search a person or vehicle with or without a legal basis under the United States Constitution or Washington State Constitution."

History was made in 2011. For the first time in any state, a bill designed to condemn and prevent motorcycle profiling passed through the legislature and into law. The dedication and efforts of the COC, US Defenders, and ABATE of Washington State resulted in success and proof that a grassroots political movement can still effectuate actual and tangible change in 21st century America.

Chapter Five

The Aftermath And The Media

*The Governor signing the motorcycle profiling bill
into law. Among everyone at the signing, the media
focused on Pigpen, calling him a Cop Killer.*

The Governor, Myself, and Twitch at the motorcycle profiling bill signing ceremony in 2011

A few days after the bill was signed I woke up to the media reporting that the Governor had taken a picture with a Cop Killer. The picture being referred to is almost identical to the photo on page 46. They were talking about my brother Pigpen. The club decided that we would answer because the truth was not being told. I was asked to write a press release that told the truth about police corruption and December 12, 1979. I prepared the following:

> Press Release: Confederation of Clubs of Washington State Re: Controversy surrounding motorcycle profiling bill signing on April 13, 2011.

> In the days following Governor Gregoire signing ESB 5242, a bill addressing motorcycle profiling, there has been controversy surrounding the fact that the Governor took a picture of the signing with a 'cop killer'. The Confederation of Clubs serves as the official voice of

motorcycle club members present at the bill signing and would like to address this controversy.

Describing Robert Christopher as a 'cop killer', instead of a victim of the most notorious law enforcement scandal in the history of Portland, is biased and unjust. On the night of December 12, 1979, members of the Portland police department and narcotics squad illegally raided the Outsiders Motorcycle Club clubhouse in Portland and officer David Crowther was shot and killed by Robert Christopher. Officers were knowingly attempting to serve an illegal warrant obtained through perjured statements about a nonexistent informant.

Narcotics officers Scott Deppe and Neil Gearhart, both present during the raid, corroborated this indisputable fact and furthermore revealed that the narcotics squad officers had come with drugs ready to plant in and around the clubhouse. In fact, it was discovered that police had planted amphetamine tablets during the raid. Narcotics officers also admitted that drugs were removed from David Crowther's pockets at the hospital after he was shot.

These are the incontrovertible facts. The entire basis for law enforcement's presence at the Outsiders clubhouse that night was to serve an illegal warrant and plant drugs. Robert Christopher was released after serving 14 months in prison because the egregious conduct of the narcotics squad was uncovered.

Robert Christopher maintains that the police did not announce themselves and that his only choice to avoid being killed was to defend himself. It was later proven that police witnesses had lied at trial when they testified that they had knocked and announced themselves. Although his death was a tragedy, David Crowther and the officers on the narcotics quad were corrupt and 58 tainted convictions were overturned before the scandal was over. Robert Christopher was defending his home and his life against an illegal intrusion and criminal conspiracy perpetrated by Portland narcotics officers.

Robert Christopher's presence at the bill signing on April 13th was understandable and appropriate. As a victim of police abuse and discrimination, Robert Christopher has put his energy into fighting for the rights and freedoms of motorcyclists because he understands firsthand the impact of law enforcement discrimination and abuse. Washington's law condemning motorcycle profiling is the first of its kind in America. Robert Christopher was vindicated and is now a free and voting citizen and had as much business as anybody in the Governor's office on April 13, 2011.

David Devereaux
Spokesperson
Confederation of Clubs
Washington State

(All claims made in this statement are based on publicly available and previously published material readily available. For example, The Oregonian, April 21, 1981, "Retrial of Christopher for killing appears doubtful." The Times-News, May 29, 1981, p.5, "Narcotics trade triggers police misconduct.")

The negative reporting ended immediately. Stopped in its tracks. NPR contacted me hoping to interview Pigpen. The interview ended up balanced, fair and told the true story. The Governor even did a televised address siding with motorcyclists by justifying our presence at the signing ceremony. The Governor basically said that it would make no sense to discriminate against motorcyclists by not allowing

Pigpen, before his release, in prison during a bike show so the brothers could come. Wouldn't see this nowadays!

them to attend a public signing of a law that addresses motorcycle profiling. The sensationalized and inaccurate reports were successfully answered. T h i s incident convinces me that a proactive approach with negative media reporting can be effective. The media will continue telling a sensationalized version of our story and the only way to even attempt to change public perception is to fight back.

Chapter Six

So Does The Law Work And Where Do We Go From Here?

Law enforcement profiling at an NCOM gathering at Four Corners, captured by Twitch, during one of our presentations.

After two years of the motorcycle profiling law in Washington, there has been a massive reduction in profiling stops statewide. This is particularly true on the west side of the state where 90% of the population resides. In fact, the only place that (at the time of this writing) seems to be an issue is the Tri-Cities area where law enforcement recently conducted a massive harassment campaign against a Confederation of Clubs meeting along with numerous other profiling stops. It is my hope that, aided with the strength of the new law, victims in all future motorcycle profiling cases are awarded financially for law enforcement discrimination.

Is the battle against discrimination and profiling in Washington State complete? Absolutely not. Not anymore than racial profiling is a thing of the past. There will always be a stigma attached to bikers in the minds of some elements of law enforcement. But the fact remains, in my estimation, motorcycle profiling stops in Washington State have been reduced by 85%-90%. And importantly, the law is legislative recognition that we are a class of people in need of the legislative protection against discrimination. Although I am not an attorney, my layman's guess is that this recognition could be very important in the judiciary as well.

A National effort to end the practice of motorcycle profiling has began. I have been traveling the country speaking and teaching about how to pass laws to address discrimination against bikers.

The word is also beginning to spread to other states. I have been traveling around the country with my brother Twitch, giving presentations, explaining the process of passing profiling legislation. As other states begin to adopt similar laws a snowball affect can be created. There are many examples of this legislative domino affect. One need only analyze how mandatory helmet laws have swung from one extreme to the other or how anti-gang enhancement laws have spread from California to the East Coast. These legislative trends, especially when backed by a strong movement, can occur rapidly and change people's lives in a real and tangible way.

My travels have exposed me to bikers from every region of America and motorcycle profiling is occurring in all of them. The North, South, East, West, and Central regions of this country all contain populations of bikers being profiled and discriminated against.

In recognition of these realities, I have started to organize an effort at the national level. The plan is to mobilize biker manpower nationwide using the US Defenders to connect all of the different elements of the movement together. The goal is to pass a motorcycle profiling law at the Federal level.

An important benefit of a national effort is gathering a pattern of evidence that can also be used by each state. As different states contribute to the national effort they are organizing the essential tools needed to pass profiling laws in their respective states.

True success would be the adoption of laws addressing the issue of motorcycle profiling on the same scale as anti-gang laws have been adopted. Law enforcement has more than enough tools at their disposal to investigate, arrest, prosecute and incarcerate gang members and criminals. Blatant discrimination against an entire class of motorcyclists based on the actions of a few is not a justifiable law enforcement strategy. All Americans should condemn this discrimination and support the movement to end motorcycle profiling nationwide.

My brother Twitch and I in Hawaii, at the NCOM
Western Regional Convention in 2011.

PART TWO

ESSAYS ADDRESSING ISSUES IMPORTANT TO THE SURVIVAL OF MOTORCYCLE CLUB CULTURE IN AMERICA

Bikers being kicked out of Oregon, Labor day 1968.

Essay One

The Elephant In The Living Room

An essay relating to what I believe to be the biggest threat to the survival of motorcycle clubs and functional brotherhoods in America. I wrote this as a prospect and am happy to say that, years later, no one in my circle is interested in hanging out with the elephant. It seems that this dysfunctional relationship can be bred out of existence.

There's an elephant in the living room that nobody wants to talk about. He has been around for so long that it's uncomfortable to discuss. Almost everyone in my community either hangs out with the elephant or has in the past. The elephant likes to party and does so for days at a time with no sleep. The elephant has a tendency to get more aggressive the longer he stays up. Sometimes he's unpredictable and begins to talk in circles. These characteristics begin to rub off on those around the elephant. In the end, one of two things usually happens. Either the person stops spending so much time with the elephant or they eventually get trampled.

I've spent significant time talking with many people who used to spend all of their time with the elephant. At first it would just be at parties. But sooner or later (usually sooner!) they found themselves consumed by their relationship with the elephant. Some of my brothers have lost everything that was important to them because of the elephant. Their jobs, their relationships, their health, their houses, their motorcycles and in extreme cases their lives. I've even had a brother locked up for years because they found trace evidence that he was with the elephant.

I've never talked to the elephant directly. But those who have in the past advise me, unequivocally and without exception, that I never should. Even my brothers that currently associate with the elephant tell me I'm smart to stay away from him. I think I'll take the advice.

Essay Two

The Day My Dad Shot Himself In The Head

An essay explaining my earliest experience and memory cementing the foundation of my belief that meth, like PCP in the '70's, is a threat to our way of life.

My earliest memory of lasting impression happened on New Year's Eve 1975. I was almost five years old and spending the evening at home with my family. My eight year-old brother, my mother, father and his two brothers were there. They were, as always, hanging out. They were part of the party generation that was the seventies.

Like most people in the seventies, drug experimentation was normal to my parents. In fact, my father was going beyond mere experimentation and involving himself in full-scale research.

On this particular evening my father decided that he wanted the dust (PCP) that his younger brother had taken from him earlier. He was already way too dusted. He was tripping out on the Moody Blues and asked his brother if he could have his shit back if he could prove that, because he believed in love, he couldn't be hurt.

Without warning my father then took a pearl-handled .22 Derringer he owned and shot himself in the head right below his temple. Amazingly it didn't kill him on the spot. (Indeed, he survived nearly thirty more years.) In fact, he calmly sat while everyone went into crisis-mode.

The ambulance was called. The cops also showed up, guns drawn, because a gunshot was involved. The most clairvoyant part of my memory is standing in front of the den's window watching them carry my father away on a stretcher. All the lights and the dramatics left an imprint that is so ingrained that I sometimes don't even realize how much this event has affected me.

One result of this memory is that I never really fucked with my father. If he could survive a gunshot to the head what was I going to be able to do to him! (In fact, the last real argument I got into with him was in 1999. At the time he was five-foot-ten and nearly 300 pounds. I was twenty-eight years old, six-foot-two and two-hundred pounds. I still told him that any dispute we have can take place at a distance of at least fifteen feet! Even as an older man I respected his extreme rate of survivability and wasn't going to allow myself to get within striking distance. After all, my father was also an intelligent man and not in the habit of raising idiots.)

The day my dad shot himself is also the day I began formulating my opinion of law enforcement. This is the day I realized being a member of this family meant keeping family business to myself. I mentioned everyone going into crisis mode. I saw my elder's fear and anxiety. I was too young to understand much of what was going on.

I did not understand the seriousness of gunshots or the drugs behind them. What I did understand, probably for the first time, was that there were two worlds in my conception of society. There were two sides to the fence. Keep the secret and keep your family safe. There is life, activity and freedom beyond the constraints of overly restrictive laws and those sent to enforce them.

I have been wary of law enforcement since 1975 and I don't see this changing anytime soon. They make me anxious and nervous even when I'm not doing anything wrong. I probably have PTSD to some degree but I have never been diagnosed. I think this incident is also the beginning of my life journey trying to understand the strength of addiction. Although my father never did dust again, he continued to drink and drug for another fifteen years after he shot himself in the head. I learned that surviving a gunshot does not immediately motivate sobriety.

I have therefore chosen my addictions wisely. I have never done coke, crack, crank, heroin or dust. Too hardcore for me I guess. I have never even been curious.

I still believe that you should have the right to do whatever you can handle. But most people I know can't handle these substances for an extended duration of time. I have seen nothing since 1976 that would do anything but confirm my early life observations.

This incident also showed me that, upon reflection and more information, our community is able to change when necessary. Dust became a thing of the past when dramatic incidents like my father's made it clear that continued use would be devastating. This proves to me that clubs have the ability to adapt and change when survival demands it.

I am positive that I will continue to reflect on the day my father shot himself for the rest of my life. He survived a gunshot to the head uniquely providing an opportunity to learn from the incident free from the dark cloud of death. I am also sure I will make more realizations in terms of the impact on my psyche. I am also very certain that my father wanted people to hear his story in hopes that they might learn something valuable.

Essay Three

The Day My Father Was Buried

An essay explaining why I think motorcycle clubs are worth saving, and why I am dedicated to the pursuit of justice and freedom for this community. Brotherhood and motorcycles.

Watching my family and father's club brothers bury him with their own hands was a defining moment in my life that will never be forgotten. The honor and respect shown by the club community to my father at his funeral is something most people will never see or experience. It turned something on inside me that made me understand my father's commitment to the club in ways I had never considered.

The brotherhood is real, heartfelt, and most importantly is centered on motorcycles. The love of riding motorcycles together is the entire foundation of the club community. The pack leading into the cemetery was comprised of patch holders from many different clubs, riding their motorcycles freely, in honor of my father's life.

Close brotherhood and the freedom of riding were so appealing and consistent with my strong sense of family and commitment to my wife and children that my desire to join the club seemed logical.

This group of strong men embraced each other without shame. These men honorably laid a brother to rest, throwing the dirt on the casket with their own hands, as if leaving such a task to a stranger would be unthinkable.

I could not have scripted a more honorable memorial to my father. I feel at peace knowing he felt honored, respected and loved. It also makes me hope I have even a fraction of the respect my father had. Maybe then my children will get to experience what I experienced the day my father was buried.

Essay Four

The Day I Learned My Role:
Speaking to the Legislature

An essay about how I found my role as a public representative of the motorcycle rights movement in Washington and the beginning of my contributions to passing a bill preventing motorcycle profiling in the state. This essay offers a more in-depth discussion of the events in Chapter 1, The COC Comes To Washington State.

I had been prospecting for exactly a week when I found my place in the club. I was given the opportunity to speak to the House Judiciary Committee at a public hearing relating to motorcycle profiling in

Washington State. This experience made me realize that my role was to use my gifts of communication to represent my club and the entire community, in defense of our rights base, because grassroots political participation is essential to our survival.

My president was scheduled to speak to the House Judiciary Committee in support of a motorcycle profiling prevention bill. Due to my communication background, I offered to help him with his speech. I spent time Wednesday drafting some ideas and was at the clubhouse bright and early, only to discover that my president had apparently come down with laryngitis and couldn't talk. I was asked if I might not be able to fill-in for him.

Absolutely. I felt honored to have earned the trust and respect that comes with representing the club. The vice president and I jumped on our motorcycles and headed to Olympia so I could speak to the legislature.

It was a trip walking into the State Capitol that first time with my patch on. I felt all the eyes on me. All the people in suits wondering what the hell we were doing.

I signed-in and we took a seat. The profiling bill was second on the agenda so we were not waiting long. Each speaker is given a maximum of two minutes. First are those in support of the bill, then those in opposition. I was scheduled to speak last in support.

As the hearing progressed it became apparent that the committee was short on patience. Every speaker was interrupted before they had reached the two-minute mark and were told things like, "Unless you have anything unique to add we are going to move on."

Although I was prepared, I have to admit that I was a little nervous when my name was called and it was my turn to speak. I was representing my club, as well as the entire club community in Washington State, and had an opportunity to speak to the individuals that implement law.

As I began, there were a few committee members writing notes and not necessarily paying close attention. Inside of twenty seconds that changed. The preconceived notion of what was expected from patch holders was being challenged. Whatever they thought, I doubt they expected the articulate, clear and well-researched presentation they were hearing and seeing. I was not interrupted.

When I was finished I could tell I had made an impact. I was asked a few questions and it was time for the opposition to testify. Two law enforcement representatives were all that showed up. They testified together and were not very well spoken. I had pre-empted their only two arguments and they were not responsive. When they finished speaking, without interruption, the hearing concluded.

I am extremely confident when I say that everyone in that room witnessed a prospective member of a motorcycle club outclass the opposition and chip away at negative biker stereotypes. My VP said he felt proud walking out of the Capitol building. I felt like I had climbed a mountain. I had just used my skill-set for the purpose of fighting for the right to not be discriminated against. An instant purpose and motivation that lives on to this day.

What happened to the profiling bill? Unfortunately, we were unable to persuade the chair, a former chief of police, and he ultimately prevented the bill from being passed out of committee in 2005. The motorcycle rights movement in Washington continued gaining strength, momentum, and I remained committed and involved. All of our efforts paid off in 2011, and we were finally successful passing a law addressing the issue of motorcycle profiling in Washington State. Nothing worthwhile comes without hard work and sacrifice. Legislative relief is no exception.

Essay Five

The NCOM Convention In Nashville: An Influential Memory As A Prospective Patch Holder

An essay reflecting my first NCOM experience and how it has influenced my goals as a patch holder and a person. This NCOM opened my eyes up to the possibilities of a unified movement based on common ground and a common struggle against stereotyping and law enforcement discrimination.

Growing up around the club is not the same as being in the club. Although it is true that you see a lot of things and learn a lot of things that someone not associated with clubs would never be exposed to, it is more true to say that you don't know shit until you are a part-of. During the end of my prospective period in the club I was given the privilege of attending the National Coalition of Motorcyclists Convention in Nashville Tennessee. During the trip I had numerous unforgettable encounters that have helped shape and determine what my goals are as a patch-holder and a person.

The first thing I have to say concerns how my president treated me at the time. I was treated with dignity and respect. Because my own prospective brothers and president were visibly respecting me, other patch holders from other clubs treated me with more seriousness and credibility. I saw how this strengthened the whole. It also laid the foundation for important interactions that would otherwise not have occurred. I was treated like a man, not a servant. This experience has influenced how respectful I am to people around me. Respect gets respect.

The second thing that comes to mind occurred during the first night at the convention. I was hanging out in the room with my president and two other patch-holders from two different clubs. My president was engaged in conversation with a fella from back east. I was standing off to the side talking to a long time patch holder from the northwest, what most people would consider a true warrior. What he said to me will stay with me forever. Maybe because what he said was unexpected. Maybe because it affirmed what I already believed.

We were talking about our kids. He told me not to listen to anyone who thought that you should put your club in front of your family. Take care of your own blood.

This is how *I* felt. Taking care of your own creates a foundation for understanding the commitment to treat brothers as if they were your blood brothers. A strong sense of family makes us better members and our families stronger.

Hearing his opinion gave me more confidence in the fact that I felt the way I felt. Especially considering my commitments to the club. They don't come much more hardcore than this man and he believed in putting your family first.

As the conversation continued the focus changed. We started to discuss fear. In fact, he was talking about a fight he got into because a brother got too close and scared him. His reaction to the fear was to strike out and smack someone.

Everyone feels fear, even the most badass mother fucker around. They might say otherwise, but fear is a natural defensive instinct. It is how you react to this fear that determines who you are. Do you run and hide or do you stand up and fight? Don't act aggressive unless aggression is what you want.

Later on the next evening my president and I were hanging out in the hospitality suite at the hotel. A jug of clear liquid was being passed around and it appeared to be having a noticeable effect on the general equilibrium of the room. I was passed the jar and took a taste. As soon as I handed the jar back to the man from Tennessee it was returned with the reply, "Now that you've tasted it, take a drink." So I took a healthy sip. Surprisingly smooth. That would be all for me.

My president starts talking to another long-time president. They are both fairly well known in the club world and I was just taking the opportunity to listen to a conversation that doesn't happen everyday. Suddenly this guy turns to me and says he wants to talk to *me* for a minute.

In a roomful of patch holders this man explained to me that younger guys don't deserve to put a patch on their back if they don't know what got us from there to here. He said he thought it was important for younger guys to understand why they get the respect that they get when they put on a patch from a club that has been around for thirty, forty or fifty years. Then he started to say that my generation held the keys to the survival of our community.

He explained that the older generation went through so much establishing themselves that they still had hatred in their hearts. Many younger guys don't yet have that same hatred so there is still the chance that clubs can mend fences and move forward. Again, this man's ideas were ones that I already agreed with. But this conversation gave me a deeper understanding of the differences between the original patch holder generation and my own. This conversation has definitely had an impact on how I view what my responsibilities and goals are as a patch holder.

Off the top, I have made learning and absorbing as much club history as I can a top priority. A lot of the narrative will never be written down. I have always been interested in the stories. I really feel that it is my responsibility to learn as much as I can.

Moreover, I don't have the hatred in my heart that may limit others. I understand that conflicts among clubs, justifiable and otherwise, fuels a media frenzy resulting in widespread fear among the general citizenry. This fear is used to justify a general crackdown on the club world. If people become scared enough our very existence can come into jeopardy. This seems to be a plain and simple truth. Unifying our efforts and resources gives us all a much better chance of surviving government scrutiny and law enforcement discrimination and abuse.

The National Coalition of Motorcyclists convention is definitely something that anyone in the club world should experience. Nearly 2000 patch holders under one roof all focused on a single purpose. One could begin to visualize a powerful constituency with nationwide reach and a unified agenda. Freedom for those committed to motorcycling.

Although I've heard a lot of criticism about NCOM's effectiveness, I have yet to see a better alternative. I also realize that any organization's effectiveness is determined by the strength and commitment of its membership. It is far easier to be negative and critical. It is much more difficult to be committed to doing the work necessary to be effective.

Essay Six

Unification as a Path to Survival: Thoughts of a Second-Generation Patch Holder

An essay arguing that unity is the best chance for the survival of motorcycle clubs in America. Conflict among clubs provides the essential fuel for government and law enforcement crusades against the biker lifestyle.

I am a second-generation member of a motorcycle club that has been around since 1968. This new generation of which I am a part faces a very different reality than the generation that started this community. In a post-9/11 world government forces are using the fear, generated by terrorism and crime, to justify and implement policies targeted at domestic entities and fringe societal groups that some feel threaten their political and social power base. It is becoming apparent that the motorcycle club community is being targeted in this culture of fear.

I believe it is the new generations primary responsibility to respect, understand and continue the path that has been created by our fathers. Political unification in the motorcycle club community is the best chance we have at long-term survival. Unification consolidates energy and focus towards the real adversary; Government policies and practices designed to dissolve the motorcycle club community based on the perception that we are violent criminals not worthy of traditional constitutional protections and freedoms.

When my father began his journey in the club scene in the early seventies the world was a different place. The United States was emerging from the conflict in Vietnam and the average age of club members was under thirty years old. Partying, fighting and riding your motorcycle took precedence over everything. Some clubs warred with each other.

Advance to the 21st century and the circumstances are very different. Although partying, fighting, and riding still receive their fair share of attention, the concept of family has persevered and strengthened. So has political participation in the form of organizations like the Confederation of Clubs. Original club members are now fathers and grandfathers. They look at the world differently. Members in their late twenties and early thirties are considered young instead of old.

Although some club conflicts continue, many relationships have begun to mend. Most importantly, 9/11 has drastically altered the social and political conditions of our general society. Change is inevitable. The only choice we have is what direction we will influence these changes.

Indeed, 9/11 has changed the very landscape of our society. Conservative forces are using the threat of terrorism to justify targeting domestic entities that they perceive as threats. The current surveillance tactics of our government are reminiscent of Hoover's surveillance of Martin Luther King Jr. and other fringe groups.

If we can be defined as warring criminal street gangs no better than terrorists then our existence is seriously in question. The culture of fear is focused on us. They are already trying to target leadership and membership of prominent clubs in the Northwest and elsewhere. The media constantly refers to motorcycle clubs as gangs in print and on television. We as a community are engaged in a war of words and perception and the price of losing is the survival of our lifestyle and enjoyment of basic freedoms.

The violent criminal street gang enhancement laws spreading across America serve as excellent examples. The legislation essentially says that if any individuals identified as members of a group of three or more people are convicted of three violent or drug felonies they are considered a violent criminal street gang. Similar to firearm enhancements, a member of a violent criminal street gang receives an enhanced sentence for any crime they commit. Encouraging membership becomes a felony.

Whether we recognize or acknowledge this conflict is immaterial. We are pivotal players in the determination of our legitimacy either through action or inaction. We will either be considered organizations deserving of Constitutional protections or criminal gangs engaged in a war against the American way of life and its security.

Our patches will either be considered examples of the protected freedoms of speech and expression or gang paraphernalia indicating membership in a criminal enterprise. This is a new time. We have a responsibility as a community and as Americans to understand these emerging realities and unify to deal with them.

Unification is a concept easier to suggest than to implement. Many warring clubs got along well enough to party with each other before problems arose. But eventually conflicts erupted between clubs because they were unable to resolve disputes that inevitably arise between strong-willed men. These conflicts have occurred in every geographical region of this country. In some cases these old disputes continue. In other cases relationships have begun to mend. Cementing these bridges and relationships into the new millennium will be, I believe, important if we hope to even partially deflect serious intrusions on our civil liberties.

Any conflict resulting in serious violence between clubs will be used as an argument to marginalize and define the entire community of motorcycle clubs as violently criminal in nature. Attempts to unify are critical because unification takes a major weapon away from an establishment seeking to target our community.

It is analogous to black rights. The civil rights movement was successful because the black community unified and verticalized their efforts. This, even if only momentarily, resulted in enough momentum to capture an historical victory. We need to learn from other marginalized communities by consolidating and focusing our energy towards thwarting the entities that threaten us instead of each other.

The newer generation of the patch holder community has the advantage of hearts clear from hatred. In most cases we were not directly affected by conflicts of the past and are therefore uniquely positioned to continue the process of unification apparent in many pockets of the patch holder world. It is my opinion that our existence as a community depends on our ability to continue building bridges of communication and common ground instead of highly publicized and media exploited conflicts among clubs. It would truly be tragic to become extinct because we allowed our anger and pride to override efforts to unify against the adversarial establishment seeking to eliminate our way of life. I am deeply committed to my club and would like to see it survive another thirty years and beyond.

Essay Seven

The Internet And The Future Of Motorcycle Clubs: An Alternative To The Mainstream Media

An essay exploring the roots of media exploitation of bikers and and the unique opportunities the internet and alternative media provides to grassroots political movements.

Although increasingly challenged, the mainstream media is relied upon as the primary source of information for the vast majority of the American population. The ability to dictate the general public's perception of reality is driven by corporate consumerism and the media's role as societies watchdog against perceived attacks on the current political structure. The mainstream media figured out long ago that the motorcycle club community was an exploitable target. Clubs are essentially anti-establishment and easily sensationalized fulfilling an American audience craving stories of outlaws, sex and violence. The mainstream media have framed motorcycle clubs as a violent threat to middle-class values that must be controlled or eliminated.

While it is true that we are currently losing the battle of perception, the war has not yet been finalized. The Internet revolution provides a more holistic account of incidents and events that are distorted by the mainstream media because both sides of a dispute have an opportunity for a voice. Motorcycle clubs have an historic opportunity to participate in the process of public perception and policy by utilizing the Internet to project our own perspective and philosophy.

It is undeniable that the mainstream media currently controls general public perception. This seems obvious and is also confirmed by research. Experts argue that the media is currently "framing our experience and forming the public consciousness of the here and now." (1)

In regards to anything considered outside the social norm, the process solidifies itself because the media is often times a person's only source of information. The general public, lacking direct access to communities and events deemed outlaw or deviant, relies on the media to shape their opinion and define their experience.

The mainstream media is "our alternative to directly experiencing the present. Imagination comprises the center of that consciousness–forming process. All individuals spontaneously form images of events in order to recognize and place them in a meaningful context.... As it applies here, it is through the media that the public's perceptions of outlaws and deviance are created and maintained."(2)

The mainstream media has controlled public perception of bikers since the original Hollister incident in 1947. The media sensationalized the event, even describing the rally as a riot, cementing the idea that bikers were essentially criminal. "Though the motorcycle had long been associated with eccentricity, Hollister created a connection between bikes and criminal behavior. Continued reporting made the connection stronger, singling out motorcyclists as an identifiable example of out–of–control youthful rebelliousness." (3)

The outlaw myth allows the mainstream media to sell its product, fulfilling its corporate function, while simultaneously promoting a general public fear of 'outlaw bikers'. "News and entertainment media, relying on myths readily understood by readers, viewers and listeners, exploited the image of outlaw bikers, identifying them early on as a menace to middle–class values. Outlaw motorcycle clubs and their activities at once served to define the boundaries of acceptable behavior, reveal the effectiveness of law enforcement procedures against a tide of criminal activity, and satisfy the reading and viewing audience's demand for sex and violence." (4) Does Sons of Absurdity come to mind? It both entertains and reinforces law enforcement stereotypes.

It is critical to recognize that the anti-establishment nature of motorcycle clubs is diametrically opposed to the media's primary goal. "In the end, what hits the page and the television screen is a pre–selected daily digest of events and opinion legitimized by the existing political structure in order to manage potential political conflict and protect the status quo." (5) This is especially true in a post-9/11 world.

The current political structure has a vested interest in sending the message that they are responding to the threats and dangers of a new world. For many years motorcycle clubs have been described by the media as a threat to society's mainstream values. Moreover, anti-establishment sentiment separates motorcycle clubs from other organizations that participate in the same behavior because they exist within the confines of the mainstream. They are part of the system that the media is intended to serve so they are not focused on with the same intensity.

So why is public perception so critical? Because the linchpin to policymaking is public opinion and America's policymakers are elected officials. If the public has enough fear of you or your community then your survival is seriously in question. As it relates to motorcycle clubs, the mainstream media's promotion of fear and violence forces bureaucrats and politicians into action. They must respond because their constituency (i.e. 'the public') demands that something be done to control this perceptual threat to society. Obviously, draconian legislation currently being applied to motorcycle clubs would meet more general public resistance if the mainstream media were not effective projecting clubs as synonymous with criminal.

It seems inevitable that motorcycle clubs will be an object of public opinion. The relevant question becomes whether clubs will start taking a participatory role in the process. Fortunately, there is a way to fight back, as individual clubs or as a community, if we so choose.

Reversing public opinion away from the current media constructed perception that motorcycle clubs are violent criminal organizations requires two distinct steps. First, motorcycle clubs must decide what they stand for in a changing world. Clubs must decide how they are different than what the mainstream portrays. Second, an alternative to the mainstream media must be embraced as the mechanism to communicate this portrayal to the general population.

A precursor to communicating is the message. The message must be formulated before it can be delivered. It is important to decide what motorcycle clubs stand for in our changing world. Not that there will ever be an across the board consensus to this question. But participating in the process by communicating ideas is critical to a true democracy.

There are many important realities about the club community that should be communicated. There are many examples. The movement towards unity in the form of the Confederation of Clubs is an historical development. Conflicts are in many cases being left in the past in favor of moving forward to protect our community as a whole. Also, emphasizing the relevance and strength of the family unit in motorcycle clubs directly challenges the notion that the community is opposed to core American values. In fact, an argument could be made that the club community understands and embraces the family unit better than the mainstream. Moreover, the vast majority of club members in the 21st century are gainfully employed. Many have defended this country and have the blood of America's enemies on their hands and their souls.

It is true that our community has experienced its fair share of sex, drugs and sometimes violence, but no more than the land-scape of American society generally. The virtues, benefits and contributions of the club community far outweigh the highly sensationalized threats being propagated by the mainstream.

Once a message has been formulated then the mechanism for communication must be decided upon. The Internet and the broadband revolution provide a viable and democratic alternative to the mainstream media. Youtube, Twitter and Facebook all represent this amazing potential. "With the inability of the mainstream media, now dominated by a handful of multinational conglomerates, to serve the public interest, and the corresponding failure of the established institutions of public broad-casting to create a genuinely *participatory* system, it is now time for more collaborative and community-based efforts." (6)

Gaining access to the mainstream media channels is not a viable option. "Because the news media cover what is new, disruptive, and threatening, they also provide publicity for alienated rebels who regard the status quo as something to be destroyed. The coverage such rebels get, however, is a mixed blessing, for it usually seeks to discredit their more extreme positions (even if they're right) while folding into the mainstream what can be carved out and held up as moderate." (7)

Only alternative media can provide a more accurate depiction of motorcycle clubs. Importantly, the curiosity surrounding our community and the currently high number of motorcycle club home pages on the world-wide web gives our community an opportunity to shape public perception and ultimately the policies that will determine our future.

Essay Bibliography

1. G. Stuart Adam, "Notes Towards a Definition of Journalism: Understanding an Old Craft as an Art Form," *The Poynter Papers: No. 2* (St. Petersburg, Florida: The Poynter Institute for Media Studies, 1993), 45

2. Dr. Ross, professor of mass communication, *Motorcycle Menace: Media Genres and the Construction of a Deviant Culture, 1997* (chapter 1)

3. Dr. Ross, (chapter 3)

4. Dr. Ross (chapter 1)

5. Dr. Ross (chapter 1) (supporting research see David Manning White, "The Gatekeeper: A Case Study in the Selection of News," *Journalism Quarterly* 27 (Fall 1950): 383–396; James Buckalew, "News Elements and Selection by Television News Editors," *Journal of Broadcasting* 14 (Winter 1969–1970): 47–54; John Dimmick, "The Gatekeeper: An Uncertainty Theory," *Journalism Monographs* 37 (1974); D. Charles Whitney and Lee Becker, "'Keeping the Gates' for Gatekeepers: The Effects of Wire News," *Journalism Quarterly* 59 (Spring 1982): 60–65; Guido Stempel, "Gatekeeping: The Mix of Topics and the Selection of News," *Journalism Quarterly* 62 (Winter 1985): 791–796; Dan Berkowitz, "Refining the Gatekeeper Metaphor for Local Television," *Journal of Broadcasting and Electronic Media* 34 (Winter 1990): 55–68. Recurrence," in *The Manufacture of News*, 64–70.)

6. Center for Digital Democracy, In Beyond Broadcast: Expanding Public Media in the Digital Age, 1996

7. Dr. Ross (chapter3)

Essay Eight

Is The Confederation Of Clubs And The Motorcycle Rights Movement Worth the Effort? Survival Says Yes.

This essay argues that the Confederation of Clubs and the National Coalition of Motorcyclists are the organizations that give clubs the best chance of combating the obvious paradigm of law enforcement discrimination and abuse.

After having been involved in the Washington Confederation of Clubs for a number of years, I have recognized that there is a perception among some that the COC is ineffective and a waste of time. There seems to be inconsistent participation from most clubs that are members of the COC. Some believe nothing of substance seems to be getting done. Others say that the

COC is a pyramid scheme for AIM attorneys to make money off of our unfortunate accidents. And I'm sure there are other criticisms. There are shortcomings in every social or political organization. There might even be truth to these statements beyond perception. But the fact remains that the COC is an historical and invaluable development in the motorcycle club community.

The political climate among clubs in the not to distant past would have made an organization like the COC impossible. No one could have imagined that the motorcycle rights movement would be among the largest in history. But as society changes so does everyone's priorities and focus. Members of the COC 'leave it on the street' during COC meetings and functions because we are gathered for a common goal and purpose. We have bigger enemies than each other.

We are vocally non-conformist and don't hide who we are. This makes us a threat to some elements in government. When we unite we take a major weapon away from them. Our violence among each other is exploited and used by bureaucrats, politicians, media and law enforcement officials to create fear among the general public citizenry. Public opinion drives policy. A scared public allows legislators and politicians to justify rights restrictive policies and huge budgets.

Consider the Patriot Act or Gitmo inmates still being held without due process rights. The attempts to label motorcycle clubs as 'gangs' or 'domestic terrorists' are widespread and well known.

The COC provides us a framework to channel our energy and knowledge among each other towards the common purpose of standing up for and protecting our basic constitutional rights of expression and assembly. Organizations like the ACLU are even taking notice of our struggles. But there can be no game if the players don't show. There is no democracy, even in a democratic society, without participation.

The world is in a constant state of social and political change. Against this inevitability there is no argument. A post-9/11 world is definitely different in terms of civil liberties and First Amendment issues. Active participation in the COC allows you to say that you participated in fighting for and protecting the liberties that define what it means to be an American, free to express and assemble around motorcycles and brotherhood.

Essay Nine

Why Do We Need A U.S. Defender Program When We Already Have A Confederation Of Clubs?

This essay argues that the US Defenders is a critical component to an effective Confederation of Clubs and motorcycle rights movement.

The Washington State Confederation of Clubs decided in early March to participate in the US Defenders. Why is the US Defenders necessary when we already have a COC and representatives from every member club? The answer is clear: the Defenders allow us to more efficiently direct our collective efforts. In essence, the US Defenders is a tool for the COC to more effectively achieve its goals. It provides a basic structure allowing each organization to place the most qualified person in charge of administrative and information gathering responsibilities. This makes information gathering more direct, immediate and accountable.

Moreover, the Defender program does not require that participating organizations be members of your COC. This allows a more widespread and comprehensive response for any call to action. Finally, the U.S. Defenders organizes all Confederations into a single network so that a response to any issue becomes possible whether it is at the state or federal level.

So why do we need a Defender when we already have a representative? It's true that in some cases the right person for a club's defender position is also the right person to be the club's COC representative. However, in many cases a club's COC representative is chosen because they can speak for their club, not because of their administrative or networking skills.

Up until the US Defenders, the Washington COC's main source of communication was at bi-monthly meetings and e-mails from our Secretary to each COC representative. This is where the breakdown occurred. Even if every representative checked their e-mail, which they don't/didn't, they would still be required to pass the information or letter on to the right person in their club. Then that information or letter would have to be returned to the representative and handed in at the next meeting. This method is frustratingly slow, inefficient and without accountability.

In comparison, the US Defenders eliminates the middleman. The most qualified administrative member is designated as a club's Defender. All communication is direct between the Commander, Lt. Commander and each Defender. By adding a structure for information gathering and immediate communication the C.O.C. becomes more efficient and therefore effective.

Accountability is achieved the moment an honorable organization agrees to participate and designates a Defender. We are judged by others depending on how well we keep our word. The Defenders becomes the manpower of the COC functioning as a tool to achieve its goals.

Independently, the US Defenders is not exclusive to COC. or club members. Any organization willing to help fight for motorcyclist's rights are welcome. Moreover, by organizing a core of independent riders (C.O.I.R.) this concept is further expanded. The COC will have broader and more comprehensive responses to legislation and other motorcycle rights issues. This puts all people with a common purpose in the same direction.

Remember, having support from regular community members and citizens increases our chances when defending our rights base. If the general citizenry is fearful and unsympathetic to bikers, then unconstitutional or discriminatory behavior from legislators and law enforcement will more likely be ignored.

Finally, the U.S. Defenders program allows an organized response at both the local and national levels. The structure of US Defenders makes it possible for a response to be coordinated and simultaneous nationwide. The more states participating the more possible this becomes. Based on what I have seen happen in Washington State, the potential of this network is virtually limitless and highly effective. The real question is, "Why wouldn't your state need the US Defenders?"

Essay Ten

September 12, 2009: The Day A Pack Of Motorcycles Captured Some Of Their Rights

This essay tells the story about the a particular day in 2009 that helped mobilize the motorcycle rights movement into the success that it is today. This essay expands upon the events in Chapter 2, 2009 A Year Of Change.

On September 12, 2009 I participated in a Washington State COC Defender protest run that gives me hope that a grassroots motorcycle rights movement can be effective. It was beautiful to see nearly 200 patch holders protesting two establishments practicing the policy of denying access to individuals wearing motorcycle club colors. There were absolutely no incidents in terms of accidents or law enforcement harassment. It was also evident that the common ground of brotherhood and the freedom to ride are more important than any differences we may have. The pack was incredible. In the end the protest was a success. The two establishments were informed of their unconstitutional behavior and changed their policies after a peaceful dialogue. I am truly proud to be involved in the mobilization of patch holders in Washington State.

Interestingly, both establishments told me their 'no colors' policies were based on the belief that the potential for violence among clubs is high even though there were no specific incidents motivating a general ban. As stated, there were zero issues among patch holders that day and almost every club in the state was represented. Indeed, the energy created by unifying resulted in a feeling of good brotherhood among everyone present. The mood was upbeat and positive and the affect has been long lasting.

What's the bottom line? The myth surrounding violence among motorcycle clubs is mostly false. The truth is that there is generally extreme respect shown among patch holders. Events like this reinforce the building momentum placing the freedom to ride above conflicts in the community. Sure there are still differences and occasional problems among clubs. But the grassroots movement in Washington State has been given priority by almost every club. So any problems that do arise are less likely to escalate. There is much better communication between clubs now than at anytime in our state's history.

Of course, you did not read or see anything about this in the mainstream media. Even regional enthusiast magazines have mentioned nothing. Wouldn't fit their stereotype. Of course there are bikers that commit crimes. There are just as many law enforcement agents and government officials committing crimes, but the coverage is more balanced because they're supposed to be the good guys. And to exclusively focus on the negative tells an inaccurate picture. This happens to all discriminated classes before they have established their rights base. So it becomes our responsibility to tell our own story.

As discussed previously, the Internet is an obvious place to begin the process. The Internet allows us to reach beyond the individuals that happened to personally witness the protest run on September 12th. For example, one of my brothers documented the day on film and created a video telling our story. Placing the video on youtube.com allows anyone to witness our success. Additionally, burning copies of the video and distributing them by hand has also helped reach individuals without computer access.

Indeed, the protest video was so popular my brother Twitch has since produced a documentary called *What it's All About*. (The documentary tells the story of the motorcycle rights movement in Washington and has been receiving positive reviews nationwide.) Utilizing available technology in the information age is essential to capitalizing on our grassroots successes.

What an important day for motorcycle clubs in Washington State. We proved that riding our motorcycles together could effectuate tangible change on our quest to secure our rights base.

Essay Eleven

December 12, 1979: A Story of Police Corruption, Imaginary Snitches, Planted Narcotics and Things You Think Only Happen On Television

This essay explains, as much as anything could, the experiences that shaped my mindset and imprinted a distrust of law enforcement actions towards motorcycle clubs. For more detail of these events refer to Chapter 5, The Aftermath And The Media.

This story is truly amazing, astonishing and frighteningly real. On the night of December 12, 1979, when I was 8, the city's drug task-force members, in plain clothes and intent on planting drugs or worse, raided the Outsiders MC clubhouse in Portland. The task-force had obtained a warrant to search for narcotics based on information they said was provided by a confidential informant.

Upon entering the clubhouse with a gun drawn and unidentified, an undercover officer was shot by a member defending his home. After a hundred and forty-four rounds were released, in response to this single shot, all of the members in the house surrendered. Every single one of them, including a pregnant woman, were physically and verbally abused and beaten. A short time later, the officer died in the hospital and our brother was charged with homicide. After trial and appeal he was sentenced to prison for killing an officer. Case closed. Or so everyone thought.

After serving a couple years in prison it appeared that there might be a light at the end of the tunnel for our brother. It turns out that one of the officers present at the raid on the clubhouse got swept up on unrelated drug charges and wanted to deal.

What this officer brought to the table shook the very foundation of Portland. Not only did the confidential informant the warrant was based on not exist, the officers also planted drugs on the scene and removed narcotics from the wounded officer at the hospital.

In fact, the drug task-force had been widely involved in drug dealing and corruption for years and countless convictions were compromised. In the end, our brother was released from prison, dozens of convictions were reversed, and fifteen officers, including the chief of police, were either fired or resigned. Truly the stuff you'd expect to find in a Hollywood action movie.

Indeed, someone should write a novel or a screenplay. It is an almost unbelievable story of corruption and perfectly demonstrates the struggle motorcycle clubs have always had with law enforcement. And they're supposed to be the 'good guys'.

Essay Twelve

A Policy Paper Addressing the Issue of Motorcycle Profiling.

The following is the policy overview I created as a tool to gain support for a bill to address the issue of motorcycle profiling in the Washington State legislature. You'll notice exhibit references that should help understand what type of evidence is persuasive. It is my hope that my work might provide a framework from which others can learn from and expand in their own states.

Motorcycle Profiling in Washington State: A Problem in Need of Legislative Relief

The Confederation of Clubs, US Defenders and ABATE of Washington State are again seeking support for legislation that would condemn and prevent the widespread law enforcement practice of motorcycle profiling. Requiring law enforcement agencies to adopt a policy preventing and condemning motorcycle profiling would reinforce the State Supreme Court's rejection of discrimination and pre-textual traffic stops reaffirming our right to privacy as outlined in Article I Section 7 of the Washington State Constitution.

I. Motorcycle Profiling by Washington Law Enforcement Agencies is Occurring and is Widespread.

¥ The Washington State Legislature's current policies define profiling in a clear and concise manner. Profiling occurs when law enforcement targets an individual exhibiting characteristics of a class that an officer believes more likely than others to commit a crime. The practice of targeting an individual because they are riding a motorcycle or wearing motorcycle paraphernalia is a perfect example of profiling. (Definition of profiling in SB 5852 passed in 2002.)

¥ Motorcycle Profiling has reached the steps of the Capitol. During Black Thursday 2009 & 2010 the

WSP indiscriminately profiled the entire motorcycle community on campus grounds.

o In 2009, the State Patrol was captured on video crawling through the bushes in order to record the license plate and identifying information of every motorcycle in the parking lot. (Video Exhibit 1) When confronted the State Patrol replied that they were gathering information based on their fictitious belief that there is always a propensity for violence when motorcycle clubs are together. (Exhibits 1,2,3 & 4, Correspondence between the Washington State Confederation of Clubs, Governor Gregoire and Chief Batiste of the WSP) This is, by definition, profiling.

o In 2010, the motorcycle constituency had to walk through a virtual gauntlet of law enforcement scrutiny in the form of personnel, vehicles and a K-9 unit before reaching the steps of the Capitol. (Video Exhibit 2)

There has never been a violent incident among motorcycle clubs at the Capitol. The State Patrols behavior chills political activism and demands legislative remedy.

¥ The Washington Courts have confirmed that the Washington State Patrol is guilty of unlawful profiling & discrimination against motorcyclists.

o In 2002, the Court granted a permanent injunction against the State Patrol's use of a training pamphlet titled BASIC BIKER 101. (Exhibit 5, Wulfekuhle v. Washington State Patrol 2002) BASIC BIKER 101 is a highly inflammatory outline of discriminatory tactics justifying and promoting abusive profiling.

o On November 23, 2009, the Washington State Patrol, under oath, explicitly admitted that they profile members of motorcycle clubs and continue to use the methods outlined in BASIC BIKER 101. The court ultimately granted a motion to dismiss all charges in the case. (Exhibit 6 & State of Washington v. James Wege 2009)

o In 2010, James Wege, a member of a local motorcycle club, was awarded a stipulated judgment of $90,000 as a result of his being a victim of civil rights abuses at the hands of the Washington State Patrol. (Exhibit 8, James Wege v. State of Washington 2010) A week after the judgment was awarded the same officer involved in Wege's case profiled and discriminated against a group of military veterans on motorcycles in Tacoma. Again, a civil rights filing is also being considered in this case. (Exhibit 9, Profiling Incident Report)

These gross violations of a Washington State Superior Court injunction and the huge settlements being awarded prove that the pattern of motorcycle profiling continues and that law enforcement in Washington brazenly violates the liberties of motorcyclists even in the face of judicial reprimand.

¥ The number of grievances and instances of profiling are continuing to proliferate. The Washington State Confederation of Clubs has gathered a substantial portion of profiling statements establishing a clear pattern of law enforcement profiling.

> o Motorcyclists are regularly interrogated about club affiliations and organizational s t r u c t u r e during what should be routine traffic stops. Almost every member of every club in Washington State (and many who are not in clubs) has experienced this type of harassment.

> o Motorcyclists are treated as an inherent threat when legally carrying a firearm with a Concealed Pistol Permit. Law enforcement has specifically identified club affiliation as justification for detainment and handcuffing during routine traffic stops out of fear for officer safety. This proves law enforcement's belief that motorcycle club members are more likely than others to commit a crime.

II. Legislative Action is Required.

¥ The Legislature is poised to act. In 2010 HB 2511 (A Bill To Address Motorcycle Profiling) passed the Washington State House of Representatives by a massive 96-2 margin. This result is a clear indication that the time has come for a policy to address the issue of discrimination and profiling against motorcyclists.

¥ Legislative action reinforces the Washington State Supreme Court's condemnation of pre- textual traffic stops and strengthens the right to privacy explicated in Article I Section 7 of the Washington State Constitution. Privacy rights in Washington State exceed the protections provided by the Fourth Amendment of the U.S. Constitution. (*State v. Ladson 1999, Attached*)

¥ Legislative action is required to restrain the State Patrol's entrenched paradigm of discrimination towards motorcyclists. The Washington State Patrol has continued to ignore the State of Washington Superior Court of Thurston County's permanent injunction against BASIC BIKER 101. Moreover, huge settlements against the State of Washington have also not been enough to trigger internal reform. The legislature has the power and responsibility to change policy when the judiciary speaks clearly and law enforcement refuses to hear.

¥ Legislative action closes loopholes that allow profiling to continue. Many times follow-ing profiling stops motorcyclists are not arrested or given a ticket. This makes it difficult to establish damages in individual instances despite the fact that it is illegal to stop someone based on a pretext. Requiring all law enforcement agencies in Washington to change their policy towards motorcyclists would close this loophole preventing less quantifiable (but no less important) infringements on privacy and equal protection.

¥ Costs would be virtually non-existent. The fiscal note attached to the SENATE BILL REPORT ESB 5852 on racial profiling passed in 2002 proves the costs of profiling legislation are negligible. More important, any costs would be outweighed by the social benefit of preserving civil liberties.

Exhibit Index

1. Black Thursday 2009 Video, DVD format, "Motorcycle Profiling in Washington State."
2. Black Thursday 2010 Video, DVD format, "Motorcycle Profiling in Washington State."
3. James Wege Profiling Stop Video, DVD format "Motorcycle Profiling in Washington State"
4. March 19, 2009 letter from Confederation of Clubs attorney Martin Fox to Governor Gregoire and Chief Batiste of the WSP concerning profiling during Black Thursday 2009.

5. March 26, 2009 response from Chief Batiste to Martin Fox justifying profiling on Black Thursday.
6. April 23, 2009 response from Martin Fox to Chief Batiste pleading for an end to the WSP's practice of motorcycle profiling.
7. June 26, 2009 letter from Martin Fox to Chief Batiste documenting ongoing incidents of profiling and discrimination against motorcyclists.
8. Wulfekuhle v. Washington State Patrol 2002, Injunction against Basic Biker 101. (Includes copy of BASIC BIKER 101)
9. Dismissal, State of Washington v. James Wege November, 2009.
10. Testimony of State Patrol trooper admitting to motorcycle profiling and the use of tactics outlined in BASIC BIKER 101, State of Washington v. Wege, November, 2009.
11. James Wege v. State of Washington 2010, Plaintiff's Original Filing.
12. Stipulated Judgement ($90,000 against the State of Washington and the Washington State Patrol), James Wege v. The State of Washington, September 20, 2010.
13. State v. Ladson 1999.

ABOUT THE AUTHOR

David "Double D" Devereaux is a motorcyclist and rights advocate primarily focused on expanding the rights base of the underrepresented. Gaining experience as spokesperson for the Washington COC, Commander of the US Defenders in Washington, National Legislative Liaison for the US Defenders, and a member of the National Coalition of Motorcyclists Legislative Task Force, David founded the Equal Protection Institute, dedicated to helping marginalized groups obtain legislative relief.